HIGH VOICE, LOW VOICE, AND PIANO

EASY CLASSICAL DUETS
18 Duets for Student Singers

COMPILED BY JOAN FREY BOYTIM

ISBN 978-1-4234-9239-9

HAL•LEONARD®
CORPORATION

7777 W. BLUEMOUND RD. P.O. BOX 13819 MILWAUKEE, WI 53213

In Australia Contact:
Hal Leonard Australia Pty. Ltd.
4 Lentara Court
Cheltenham, Victoria, 3192 Australia
Email: ausadmin@halleonard.com.au

Visit Hal Leonard Online at
www.halleonard.com

PREFACE

Duet singing in the private voice studio can add a valuable dimension to the musical experiences of the teenage student, as well as the typical community adult singer. Many benefits include the pure joy of singing with another person using a similar vocal technique, learning to tune to another voice in the same basic range or a contrasting range, becoming an independent singer in a contrapuntal line against the main melody, and feeling the expressive nuances developed through compromising "give and take" phrasing.

For many years before students became so involved in sports and so many extra curricular activities, I had many active duet pairs in my studio. It is much more difficult these days. However, I presently have two sisters and two brothers working together, plus several school friends. Because of a lack of books with enough suitable material, in the past I have had to use mainly two-part choral octavos.

This duet volume is intended to introduce many unfamiliar and previously out of print secular songs of easy to moderate difficulty. In addition to appealing to students and duet pairs, these songs will provide the opportunity for continual musical growth.

The very easy, "All Through the Night," "Morning," "Sweet and Low," "When Twilight Weaves," and "A Poor Soul Sat Sighing," are set in typical two-part style, with some particularly interesting moving parts. "Come to the Fair" and "May Day Carol" are very familiar songs loved by singers of all ages. "About Katy" and "Nearest and Dearest" show some subtle humor.

Slightly more difficult with more melismatic style writing are "The Day Is Fair," "In Springtime," "The Time of Youth," and "Trip It in a Ring." Beautiful expressive lines are prominent in "Who Is Sylvia?" and "Only to Thee" (a setting of the Saint-Saëns "The Swan").

This volume of 18 secular duets should provide new experiences for teachers and students interested in duet repertoire.

Joan Frey Boytim
June, 2010

CONTENTS

ABOUT KATY

Edith Sanford Tillotson

Ira B. Wilson

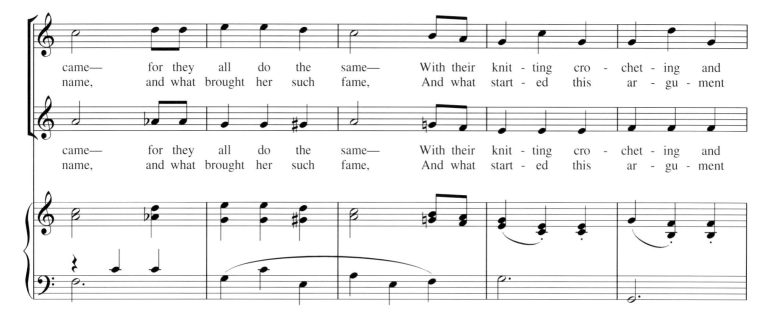

came— for they all do the same— With their knit - ting cro - chet - ing and
name, and what brought her such fame, And what start - ed this ar - gu - ment

came— for they all do the same— With their knit - ting cro - chet - ing and
name, and what brought her such fame, And what start - ed this ar - gu - ment

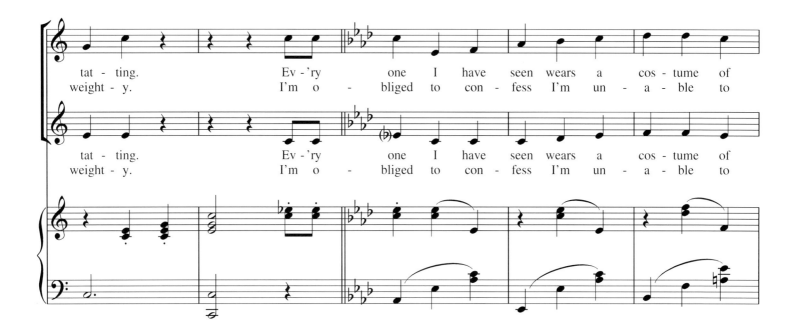

tat - ting. Ev - 'ry one I have seen wears a cos - tume of
weight - y. I'm o - bliged to con - fess I'm un - a - ble to

tat - ting. Ev - 'ry one I have seen wears a cos - tume of
weight - y. I'm o - bliged to con - fess I'm un - a - ble to

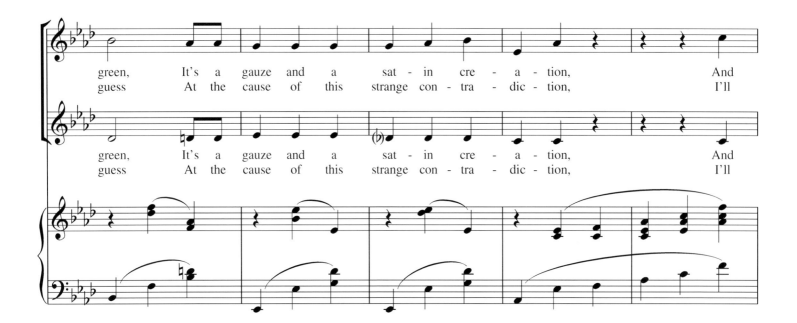

green, It's a gauze and a sat - in cre - a - tion, And
guess At the cause of this strange con - tra - dic - tion, I'll

green, It's a gauze and a sat - in cre - a - tion, And
guess At the cause of this strange con - tra - dic - tion, I'll

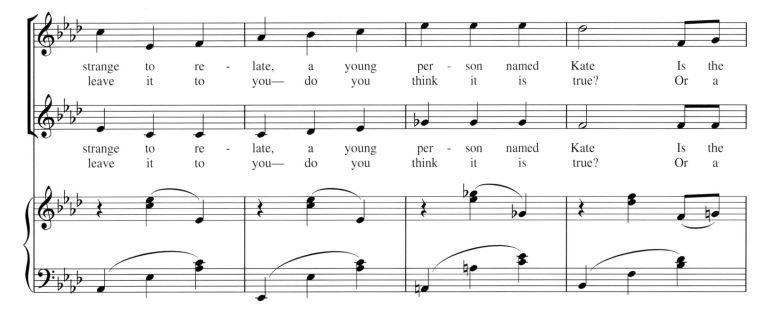

She did-n't she did-n't, She did-n't, she did-n't, she

did, Ka-ty did, Ka-ty did, Ka-ty did, She did, she did, she

did-n't, she did-n't— This whole af-ter-noon they clung to that tune, And it

did, she did— This whole af-ter-noon they clung to that tune, And it

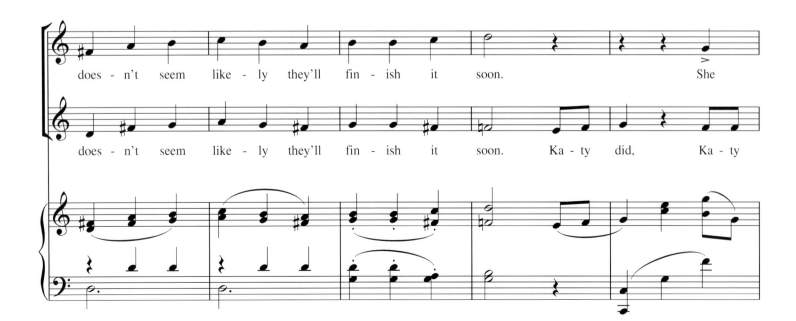

does-n't seem like-ly they'll fin-ish it soon. She

does-n't seem like-ly they'll fin-ish it soon. Ka-ty did, Ka-ty

did-n't,   she did-n't,   She did-n't, she did-n't, she

did,   Ka-ty did,   Ka-ty did,   She did, she did, she

did-n't,   she did-n't,   I'd love to find out what they're talk-ing a-

did,   she did,   I'd love to find out what they're talk-ing a-

bout, And to know what she did   or she did-n't.

bout, And to know what she did   or she did-n't.

ALL THROUGH THE NIGHT

Harold Boulton

Old Welsh Melody
Arranged by N. Clifford Page

Soft the drows - y hours are creep - ing, Hill and vale in
Love's young dream, a - las is o - ver, Yet my strains of

slum - ber sleep - ing, Love a - lone his watch is keep - ing,
love shall hov - er, Near the pres - ence of my lov - er,

All thro' the night.
All thro' the night.

Meno mosso e poco tranquillamente

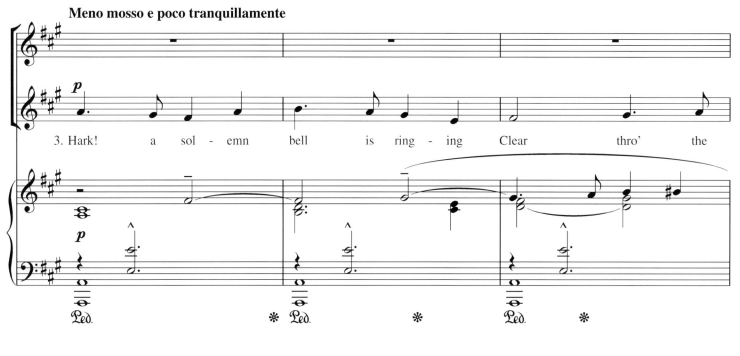

3. Hark! a sol - emn bell is ring - ing Clear thro' the

night. Thou, my love, art heav'n - ward wing - ing

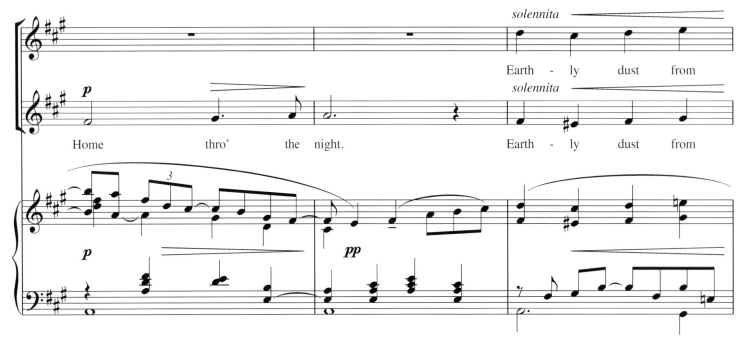

Earth - ly dust from
Home thro' the night. Earth - ly dust from

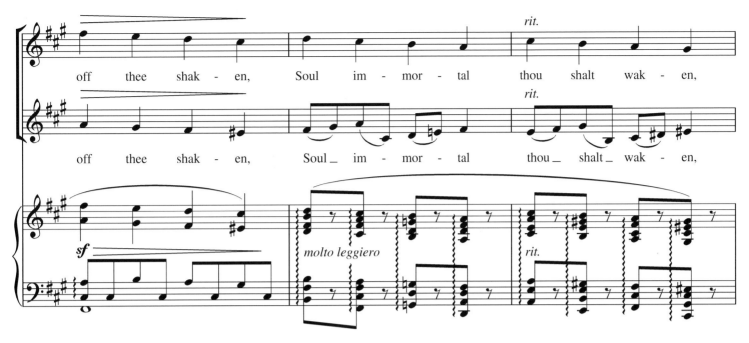

off thee shak - en, Soul im - mor - tal thou shalt wak - en,

off thee shak - en, Soul im - mor - tal thou shalt wak - en,

With thy last dim jour - ney tak - en, Home thro' the

With thy last dim jour - ney tak - en, Home thro' the

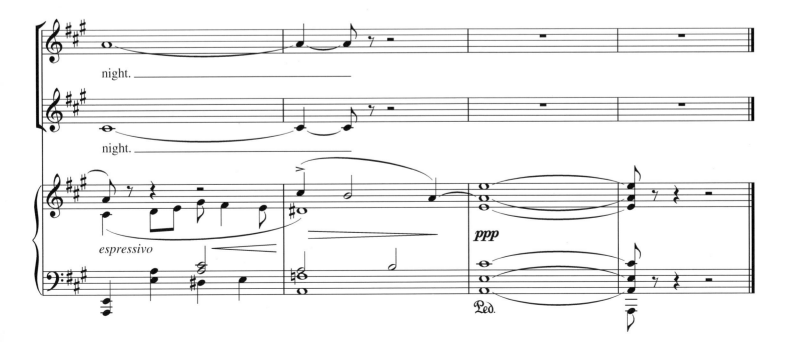

night.

night.

COME TO THE FAIR
from *Three More Songs of the Fair*

Helen Taylor

Easthope Martin
Arranged as a duet

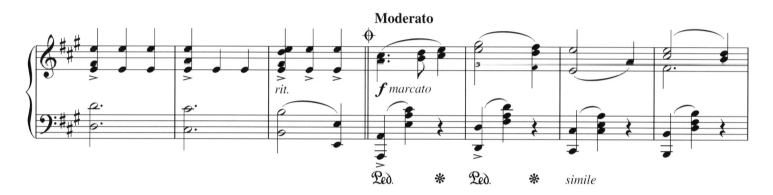

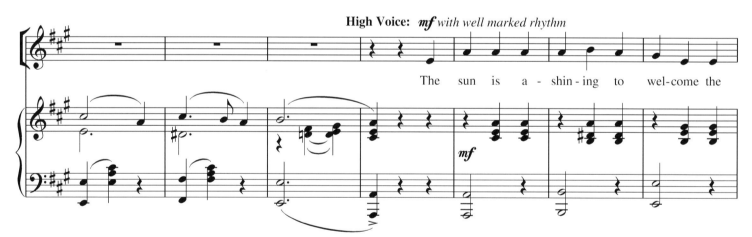

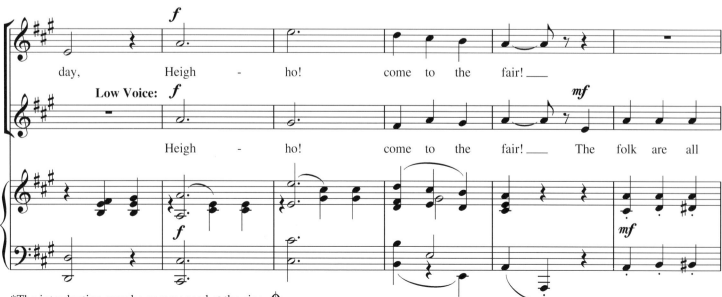

*The introduction may be commenced at the sign ⊕

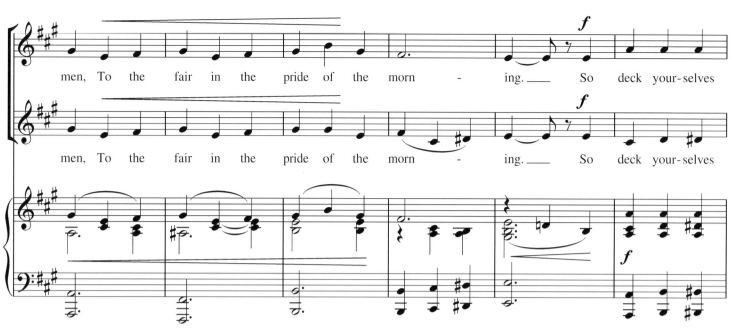

men, To the fair in the pride of the morn - ing. ___ So deck your-selves

men, To the fair in the pride of the morn - ing. ___ So deck your-selves

out in your fin - est ar - ray, With a heigh - ho! ___

out in your fin - est ar - ray, With a heigh - ho! ___

come to the fair! ___

come to the fair! ___

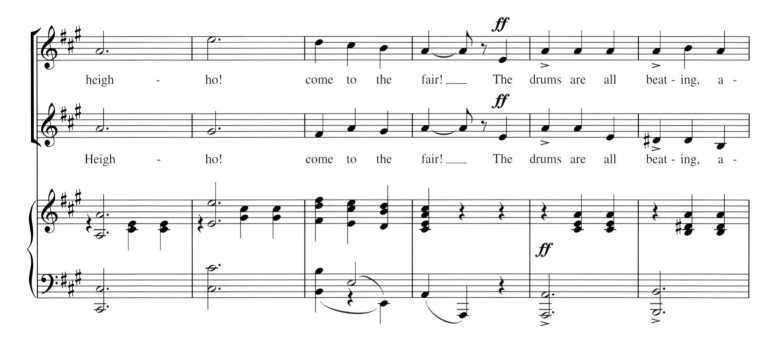

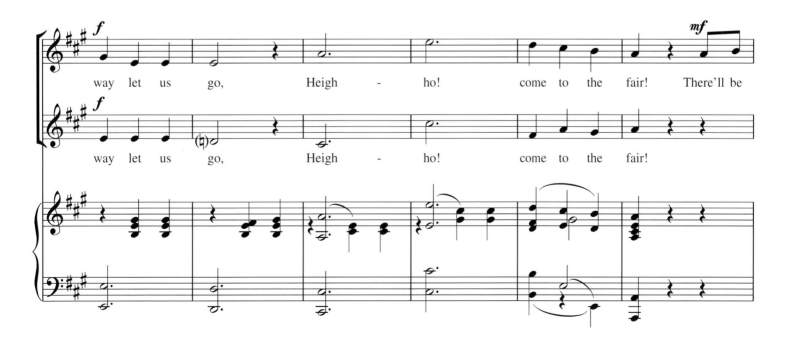

rac-ing   from morn-ing   And round-a-bouts turn-ing

and chas-ing   till night, __   to

riten. , *ten.* *ten.* **f** *a tempo*   *mf*

So it's come   then,   maid-ens and men, To the

, *ten.* *ten.* **f** *a tempo*   *mf*

left and to right, So it's come   then,   maid-ens and men, To the

riten. **f** *a tempo*   *mf*

mf

fair in the pride of the morn -   ing. __ So lock up your house, there'll be

mf

fair in the pride of the morn -   ing. __ So lock up your house, there'll be

mf

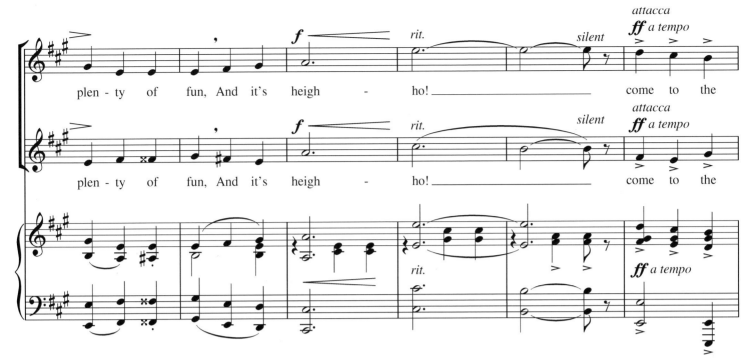

plen - ty of fun, And it's heigh - ho! _____ come to the

plen - ty of fun, And it's heigh - ho! _____ come to the

fair! _____

fair! _____

For love mak - ing if you've a mind, _____

For love mak - ing, too, if so be you've a mind, _____

Heigh - ho! come to the fair! For hearts that are hap-py are

Heigh - ho! come to the fair! For hearts that are hap-py are

lov - ing and kind, Heigh - ho! come to the fair! If

lov - ing and kind, Heigh - ho! come to the fair! If

"Haste to the wed-ding" the fid - dles should play, I'll war - rant you'll dance to the

"Haste to the wed-ding" the fid - dles should play, I'll war - rant you'll dance to the

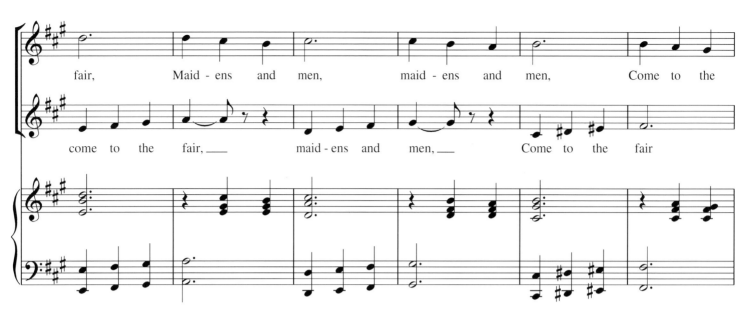

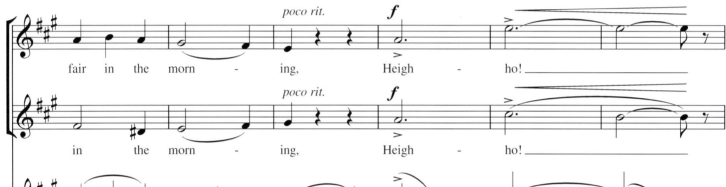

IN SPRINGTIME

William Shakespeare

Ernest Newton

Allegretto

High Voice:

It was a lov - er and his lass, With a hey and a ho, and a hey non-i - no, That

o'er the green corn - field did pass, In the spring - time, in the spring - time, in the

spring - time, in the spring - time, the on - ly pret - ty, pret - ty

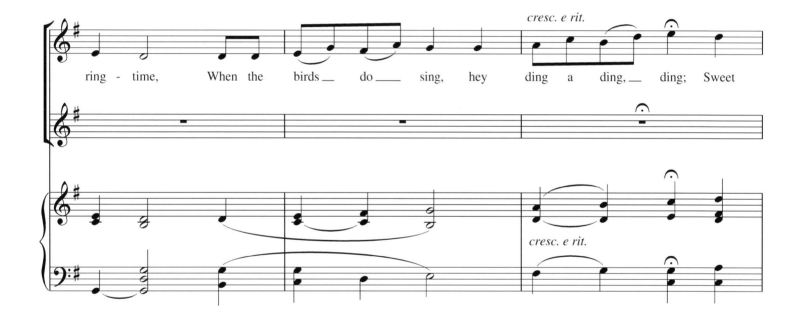

cresc. e rit.

ring - time, When the birds do sing, hey ding a ding, ding; Sweet

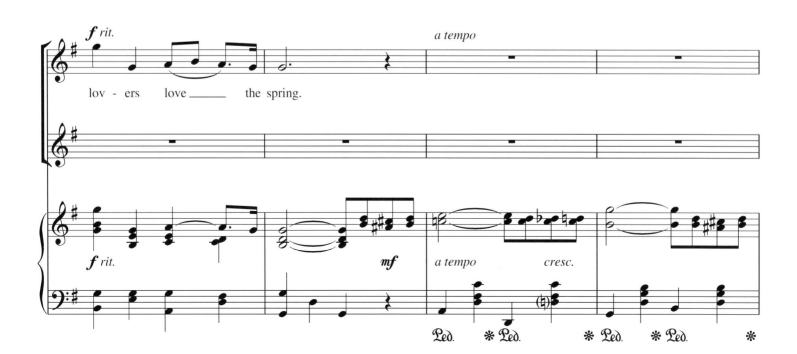

f *rit.*   *a tempo*

lov - ers love the spring.

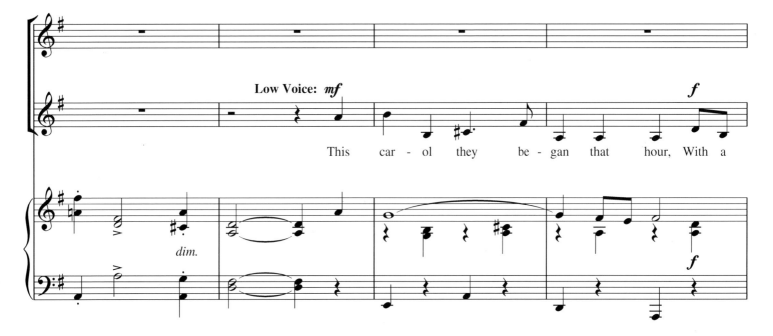

Low Voice: *mf* ... *f*

This car - ol they be - gan that hour, With a

dim. *f*

hey and a ho, and a hey non - i - no, How that a life is

p

but a flow'r, In the spring - time, in the spring - time, in the

cresc. *rit.* *mf a tempo*

spring - time, in the spring - time, the on - ly pret - ty, pret - ty

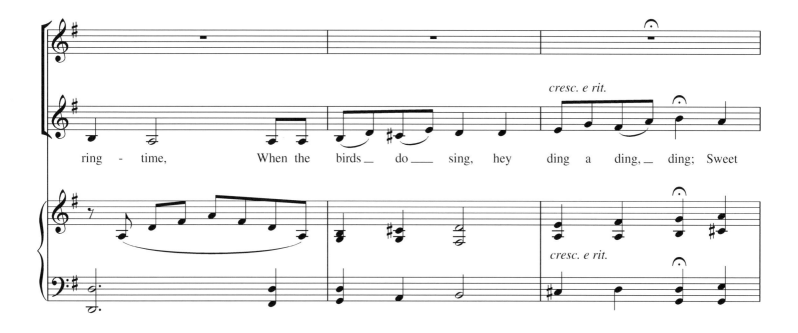

ring - time, When the birds do sing, hey ding a ding, ding; Sweet

cresc. e rit.

And

lov - ers love the spring.

there - fore take the pre - sent time, With a hey and a ho, and a

And there - fore take the pre - sent time, With a hey and a ho, and a

hey non - i - no; For love is crown - ed with the prime, In the

hey non - i - no; For love is crown - ed with the prime, In the

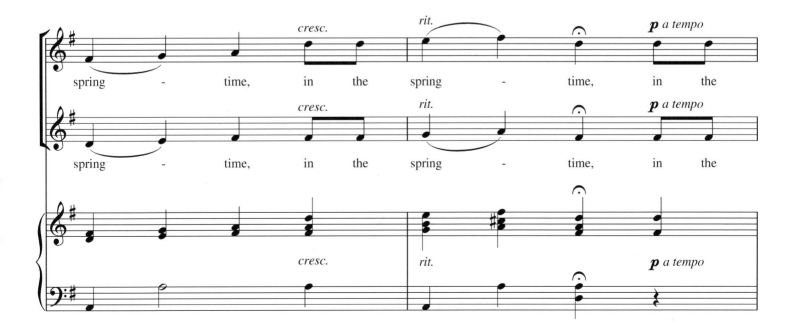

spring - time, in the spring - time, in the

spring - time, in the spring - time, in the

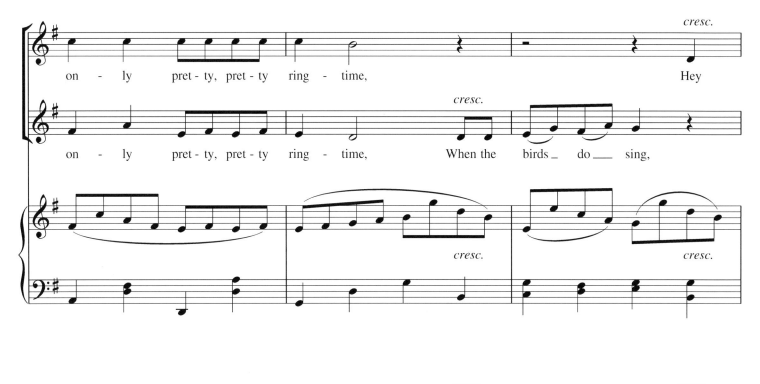

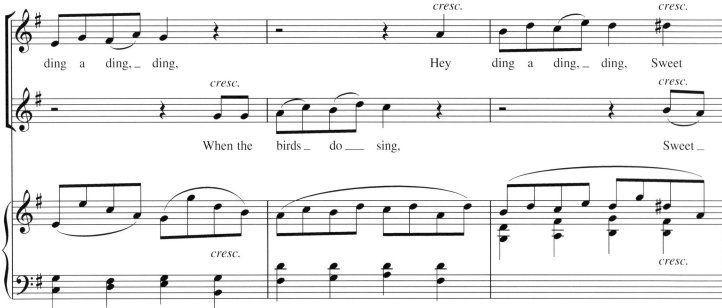

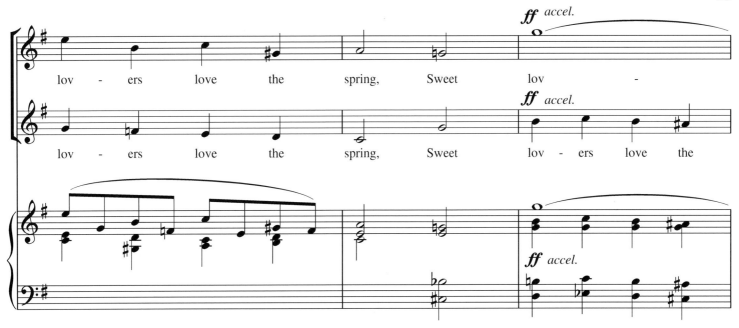

lov - ers love the spring, Sweet lov -

lov - ers love the spring, Sweet lov - ers love the

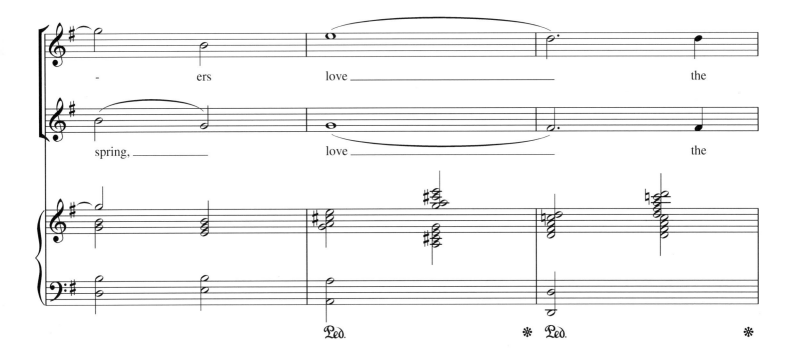

- ers love _____ the

spring, _____ love _____ the

spring. _____

spring. _____

THE DAY IS FAIR
(Pastorale)

Siegfried Swenson

Lily Strickland

Allegro

la, _____ tra la, _____ tra la! _____ How

sweet __ is love in spring!

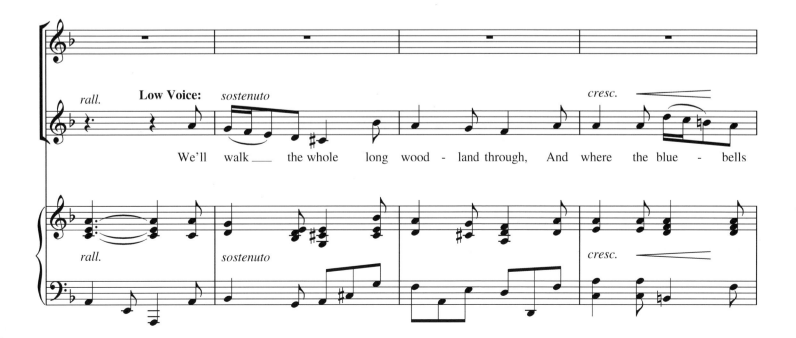

We'll walk __ the whole long wood - land through, And where the blue - bells

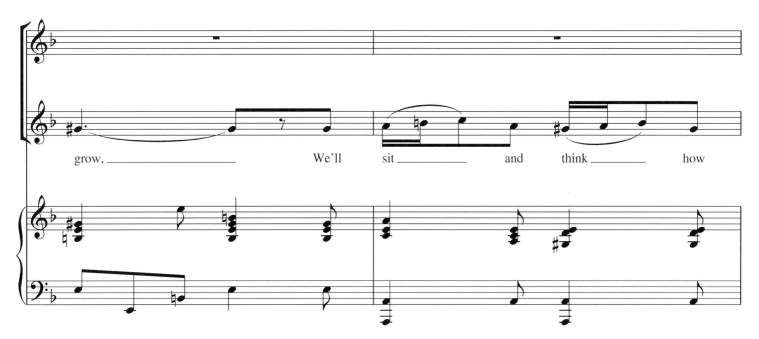

grow, _____ We'll sit _____ and think _____ how

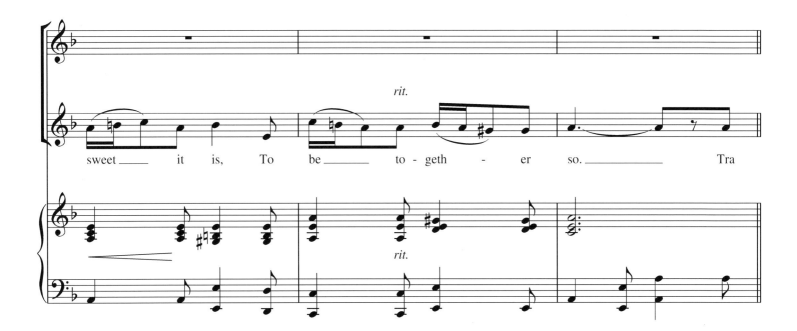

sweet ___ it is, To be ___ to - geth - er so. _____ Tra

Allegro

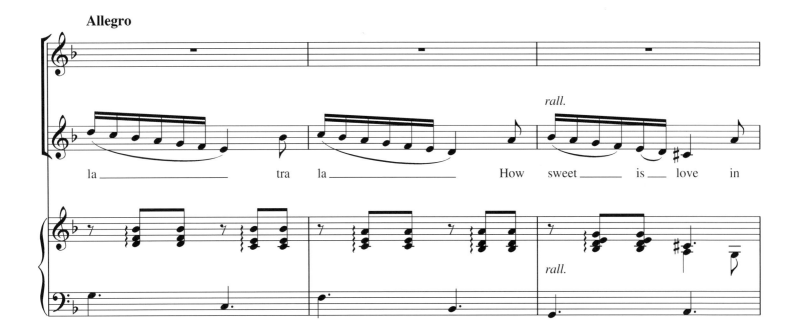

la _____ tra la _____ How sweet ___ is ___ love in

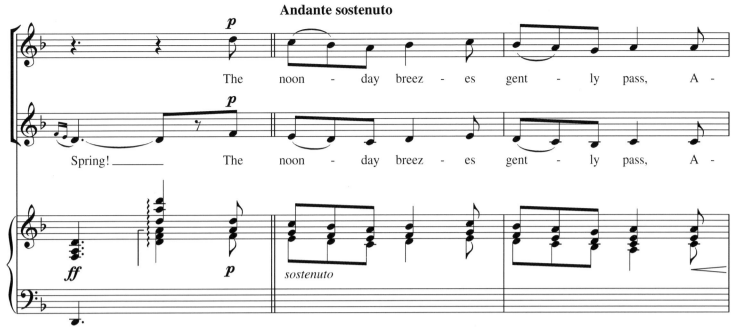

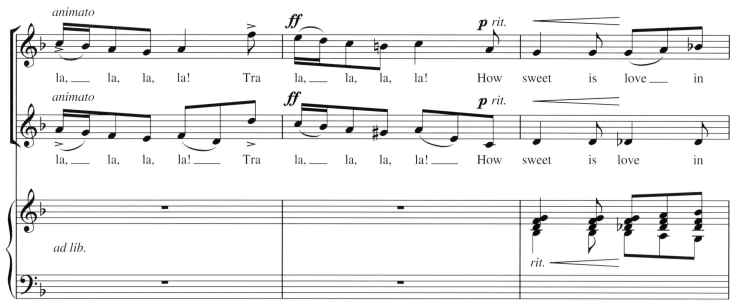

la, la, la, la! Tra la, la, la, la! How sweet is love in
la, la, la, la! Tra la, la, la, la! How sweet is love in

Spring! 'Til light of day doth leave the sky, We
Spring! 'Til light of day doth leave the sky, We

wan - der in the field, And pluck the flow - ers
wan - der in the field, And pluck the flow - ers

bloom - ing there, And prize __ the scents __ they yield. _____ And

bloom - ing there, And prize __ the scents __ they yield. _____ And

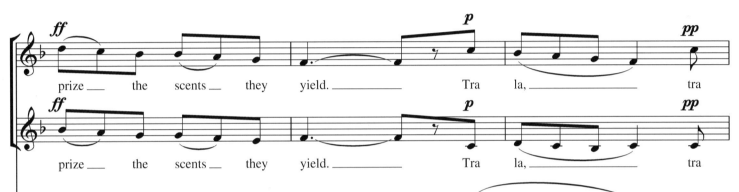

prize __ the scents __ they yield. _____ Tra la, _____ tra

prize __ the scents __ they yield. _____ Tra la, _____ tra

la _____ How sweet __ is love __ in Spring.

la _____ How sweet __ is love __ in Spring.

FROM FAR AWAY
from *Tuscan Folk Songs*, No. 2

Luigi Caracciolo

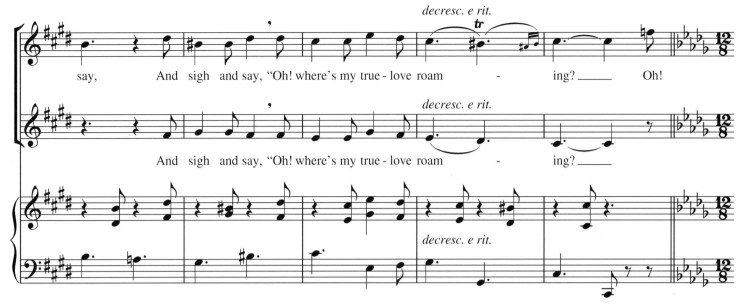

un poco meno mosso

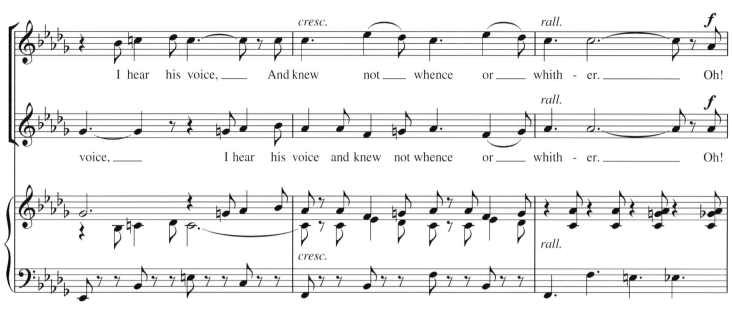

I hear his voice, ____ And knew not ____ whence or ____ whith - er. _____ Oh!

voice, ____ I hear his voice and knew not whence or ____ whith - er. _____ Oh!

where's my true - love roam - ing, far - ther, near - er? Oh! where's my true - love roam - ing, far - ther

where's my true - love roam - ing, far - ther, near - er? Oh! where's my true - love roam - ing, far - ther

near - er? Oh! where's he roam - ing? Oh! where's he roam - ing? When

near - er? Oh! where's he roam - ing? Oh! where's he roam - ing? When

none in all the world can love him dear - er! Oh! where's he

none in all the world can love him dear - er! Oh! where's he

roam - ing? When none in all the world can love him dear - er. Oh! there's none can love him

roam - ing? When none in all the world can love him dear - er. Oh! there's none can love him

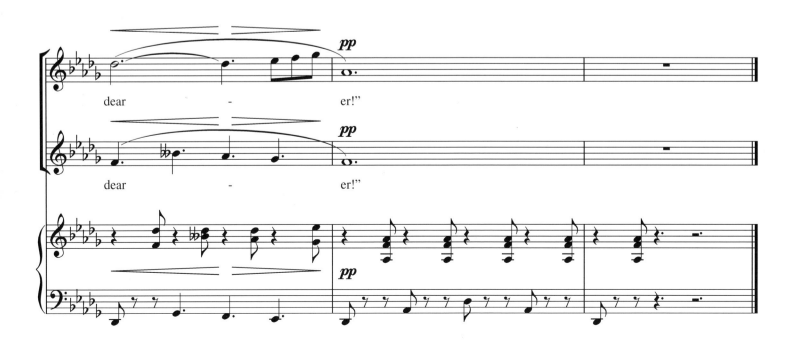

dear - er!"

dear - er!"

LET US WANDER
from *The Indian Queen*

John Milton from L'Allegro
Adapted by Alfred Moffat

Henry Purcell
Arranged by Alfred Moffat

elms, on hil - locks _ green, While the _ plough - man, _ near _ at _

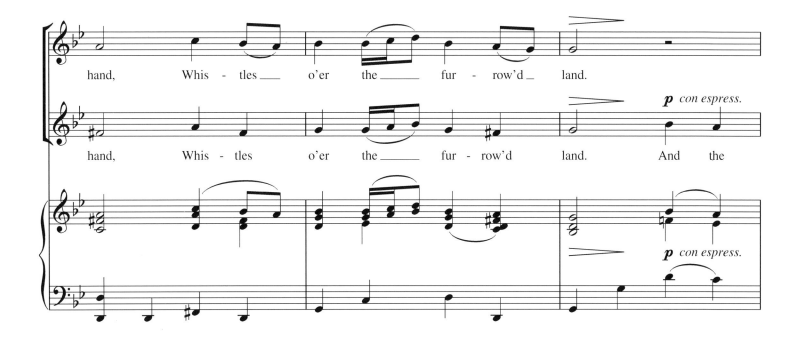

hand, Whis - tles _ o'er the _ fur - row'd _ land.

hand, Whis - tles o'er the _ fur - row'd land. And the

p con espress.

p con espress.

And the shep - herd tells _ his _ tale, Be -

shep - herd, and the shep - herd tells _ his _ tale, Be -

pp

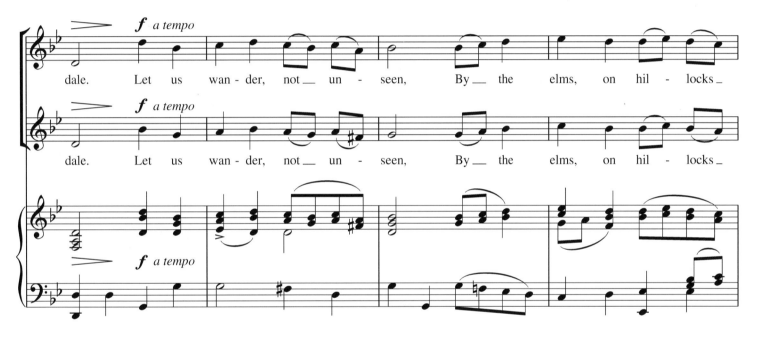

MAY DAY CAROL
(English Folksong)

Air from Essex County
Arranged by Deems Taylor

42

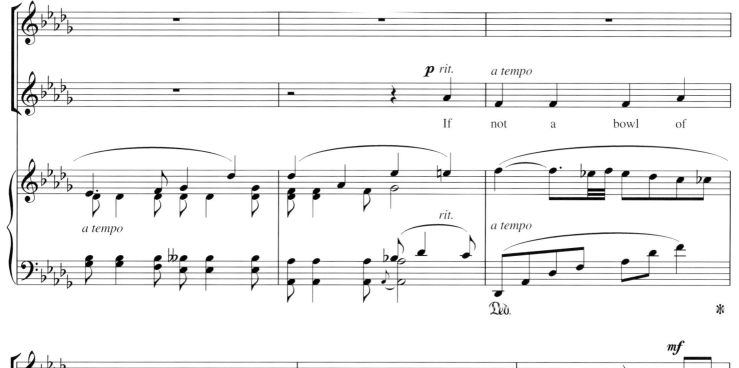

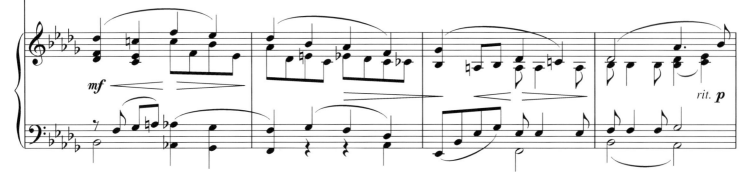

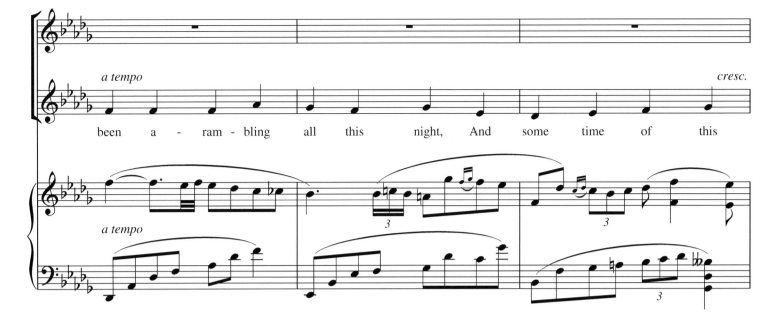

been a - ram - bling all this night, And some time of this

And now, re - turn - ing

day, And now, re - turn - ing

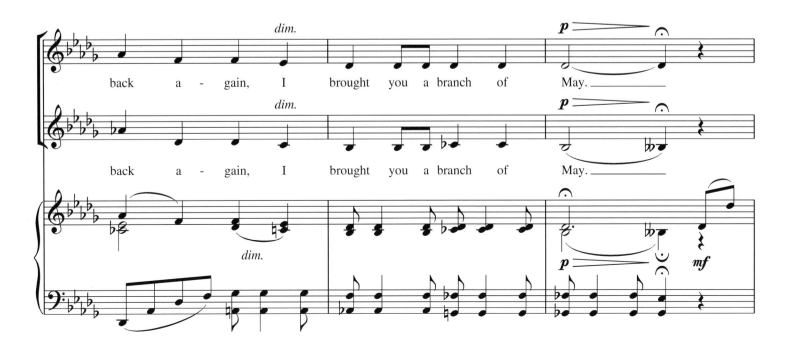

back a - gain, I brought you a branch of May.

back a - gain, I brought you a branch of May.

MORNING

from *Peer Gynt Suite*, Op. 46, No. 1

E. M. Carroll

Edvard Grieg
Arranged by Christopher O'Hare

with sweet-est mirth, Hail the morn - ing,

with sweet-est mirth, Hail thee, hail, Oh,

All earth with

bright - est morn - ing, All earth with

glo - ry a - dorn - ing. Bright on the world, Now the

glo - ry a - dorn - ing. Now, in

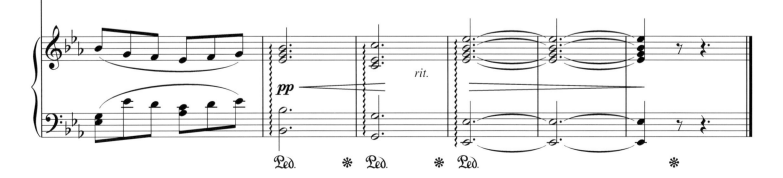

NEAREST AND DEAREST

from *Tuscan Folk Songs*, No. 6

Luigi Caracciolo

Then thou art dear - er! Ah! _____

Then thou art dear - er! Ah! _____

p

p

p con brio

Yet Sat - ur - day we've

Now Fri - day's here, I think my love is sweet - est,

52

vow'd shall be the one day. Ah, yes my

When Sun-day comes we walk in all our neat-est.

love is near-er, dear-er Sun-day! Then thou art near-est,

Then thou art near-est,

Then thou art dear-est! Ah! _____

Then thou art dear-est! Ah! _____

Then thou art near - est

Then thou art near - est

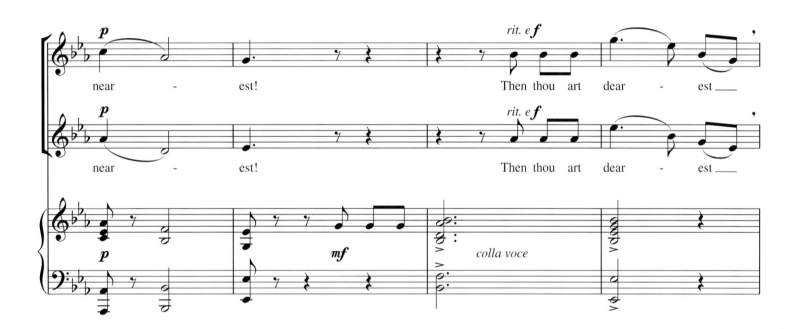

near - est!

near - est!

Then thou art dear - est___

Then thou art dear - est___

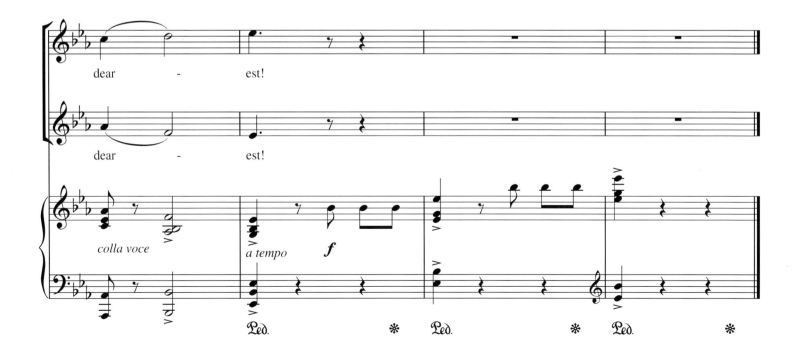

dear - est!

dear - est!

ONLY TO THEE

Gena Branscombe

Camille Saint-Saëns
Arranged by Gena Branscombe

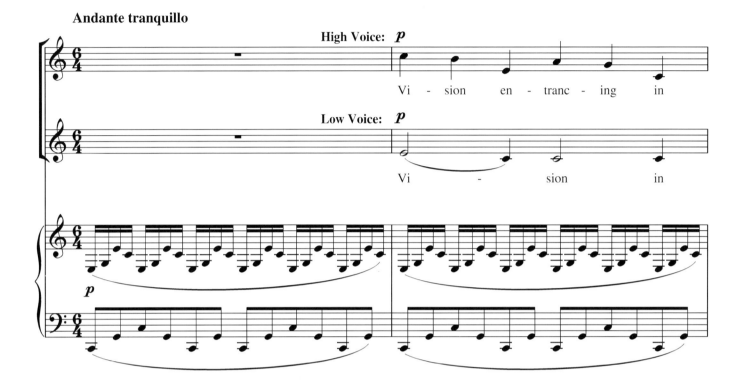

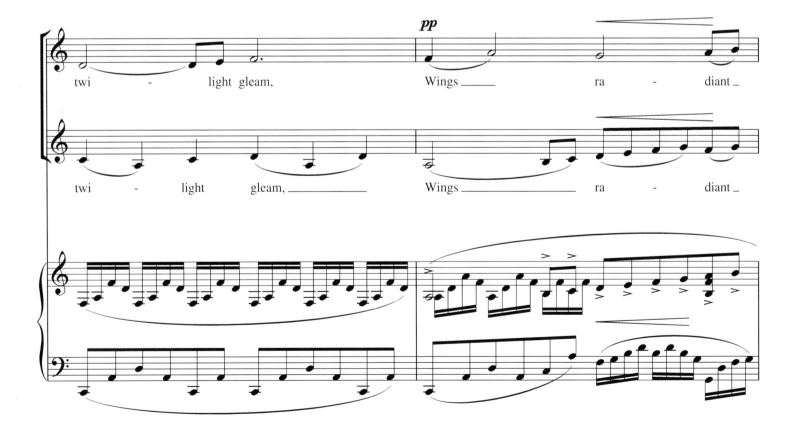

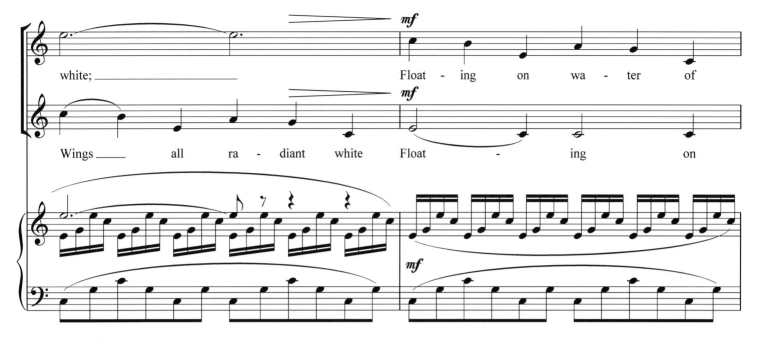

glo - ry fade, Ling - 'ring in beau - ty while

Love, nev - er more will the glo - ry fade, _____

life _____ shall last; Ech - oes of mel - o - dy

Ling - 'ring in beau - ty while life shall last; _____

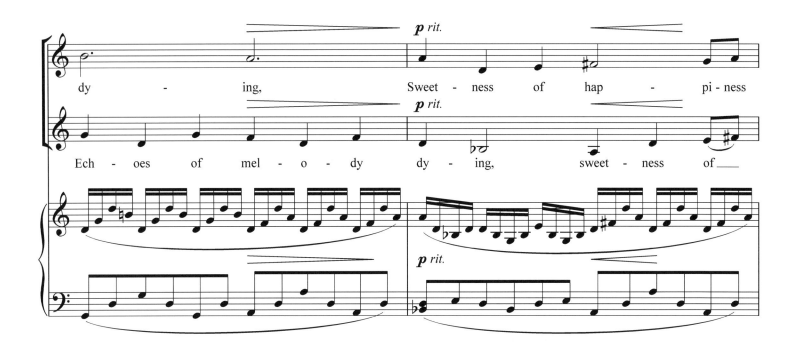

dy - ing, Sweet - ness of hap - pi - ness

Ech - oes of mel - o - dy dy - ing, sweet - ness of ____

p rit.

THE TIME OF YOUTH

Charles J. Rowe

Ciro Pinsuti

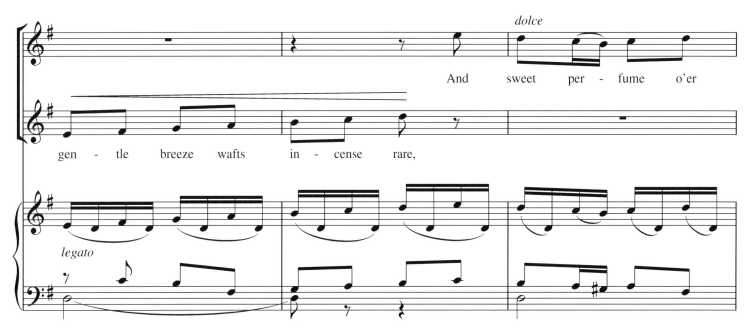

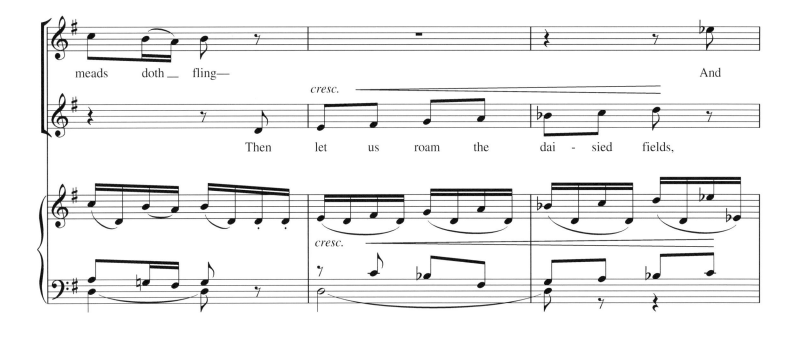

let us roam the dai - sied fields, And wel - come in the love - ly Spring, And

let us roam the dai - sied fields, And wel - come in the love - ly Spring, And

wel - come in _____ the _ love-ly, _ love-ly _ Spring, _____ And wel - come

wel - come in _____ the _ love-ly, _ love-ly _ Spring, _____ And wel - come

in _____ the _ love - ly, _ love - ly Spring!

in _____ the _ love - ly, _ love - ly Spring!

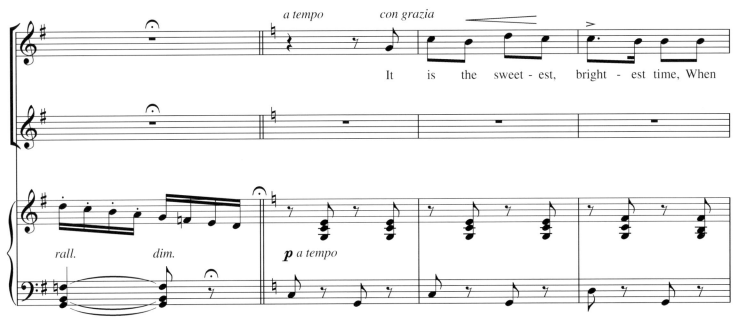

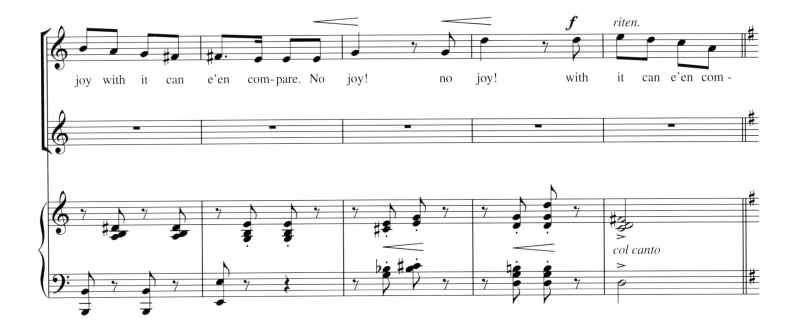

Then let us roam the fresh, green fields And hear the fea-ther'd cho-rus sing, A

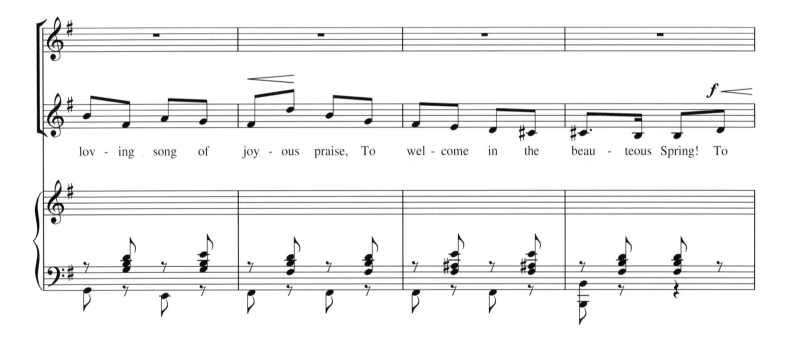

lov-ing song of joy-ous praise, To wel-come in the beau-teous Spring! To

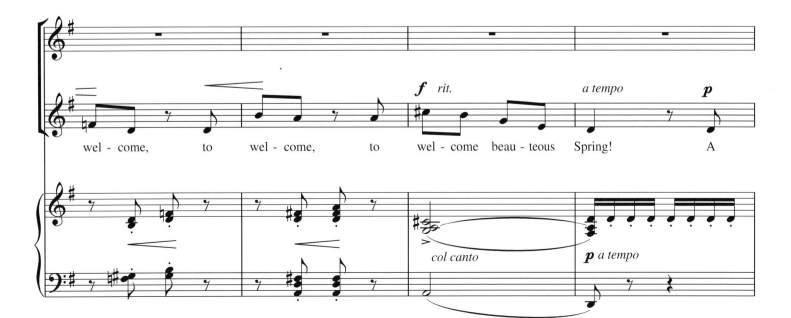

wel-come, to wel-come, to wel-come beau-teous Spring! A

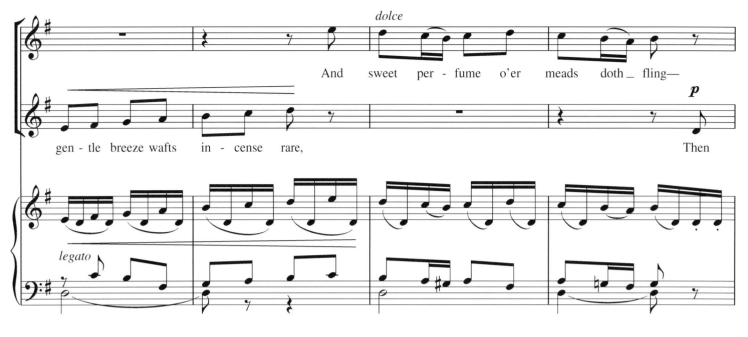

hear the fea - ther'd cho - rus sing, A lov - ing song ___ of ___

hear the fea - ther'd cho - rus sing, A lov - ing song ___ of ___

joy - ous, _ joy - ous _ praise, ___ To wel - come in ___ the ___

joy - ous, _ joy - ous _ praise, ___ To wel - come in ___ the ___

beau - teous, beau - teous Spring!

beau - teous, beau - teous Spring!

A POOR SOUL SAT SIGHING

William Shakespeare
from *Othello*

Mary Carmichael

67

Her salt tears fell
by __ her and mur-mur'd __ her moans; Her salt tears fell

from her and soft - ened the stones;
from her and soft - ened the stones;

Sing wil - low, __ wil - low, Sing wil - low, __
Sing wil - low, __ wil - low, Sing wil - low, __

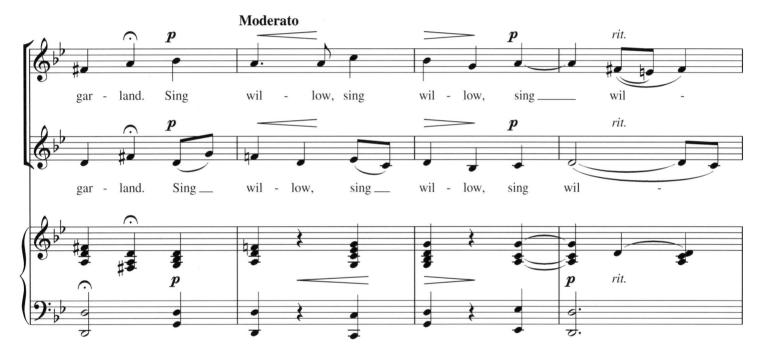

SPRING–SONG
(Frühlingslied)

Emanuel von Geibel
English version by James D. Trenor

Eduard Lassen

Slowly, with tenderness
Langsam, zart vorgetragen

High Voice:

Tief im grü - nen Früh - lings-
Deep the spring clad glades a -

Low Voice:

Tief im grü - nen Früh - lings-
Deep the spring clad glades a -

hag durch die al - ten Rü - stern
mong 'mid the a - ged beech - es

hag durch die al - ten Rü - stern
mong 'mid the a - ged beech - es

wan - delt leis am schön - sten Tag._____
*Mys - tic whisp - 'rings soft - ly steal*_____

wan - delt leis am schön - sten Tag._____
*Mys - tic whisp - 'rings soft - ly steal*_____

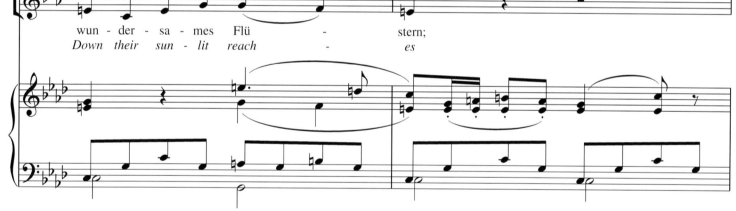

wun - der - sa - mes Flü - stern;
Down their sun - lit reach - es

wun - der - sa - mes Flü - stern;
Down their sun - lit reach - es

meno **p**   **pp**

je - des Läub - lein spricht: Gott grüss! zu dem Laub da - ne - ben.
Not a plant but says   God - speed to its glad - some neigh - bor

meno **p**   **pp**

je - des Läub - lein spricht: Gott grüss! zu dem Laub da - ne - ben.
Not a plant but says   God - speed to its glad - some neigh - bor

meno **p**   **pp**

Al - les ath - met tief und süss Heil'- ges Frie - dens - le - ben,
All a - round breathes deep and sweet Life with - out life's la - bor:

Al - les ath - met tief und süss Heil'- ges Frie - dens - le - ben,
All a - round breathes deep and sweet Life with - out life's la - bor:

und wie Blüth' und Blatt am Strauch
and as sway - ing bud and leaf

und wie Blüth' und Blatt am Strauch
and as sway - ing bud and leaf

still sich wiegt im Glan - ze
Sun's bright beam in - vad - eth

still sich wiegt im Glan - ze
Sun's bright beam in - vad - eth

wiegt sich mei - ne Seel' im Hauch, der ___ durch -
Sways my in - most soul the Breath which ___ the ___

wiegt ___ sich mei - ne Seel' im Hauch, der ___ durch -
Sways ___ my in - most soul the Breath which ___ the ___

strömt _ das ___ Gan - ze.
whole _ per - vad - eth.

strömt _ das Gan - ze.
whole _ per - vad - eth.

SWEET AND LOW
(A Lullaby)

Lord Alfred Tennyson

Joseph Barnby
Arranged by John E. West

Over the roll - ing wa - ters go, Come from the dy - ing moon __ and blow,

O - ver the wa - ters go, Come from the moon __ and blow,

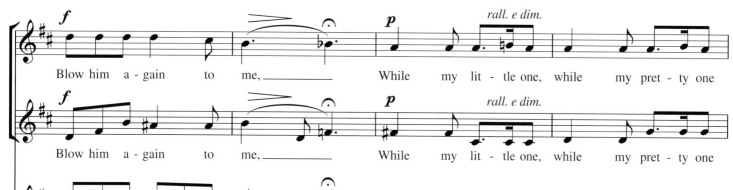

Blow him a - gain to me, _____ While my lit - tle one, while my pret - ty one

Blow him a - gain to me, _____ While my lit - tle one, while my pret - ty one

sleeps. _____

sleeps. _____

TRIP IT IN A RING
from *The Fairy Queen*

Edmund Spencer

Henry Purcell
Adapted as a duet
Accompaniment by Joel K. Boyd

sing, dance and sing, a - round,_____ a - round,_____ a-

round _____ this mor - tal dance _ and _ sing, this

a - round _____ this mor - tal dance and sing, this

mor - tal dance _ and _ sing. Trip it, mor - tal dance _ and _ sing.

mor - tal dance and sing. Trip it, mor - tal dance and sing.

* Play cue notes 2nd time.

WHEN TWILIGHT WEAVES
(Minuet)

Gena Branscombe

Ludwig van Beethoven
Arranged by Gena Branscombe

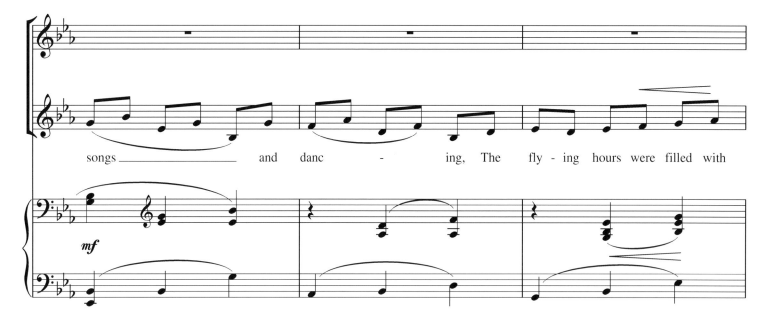

songs _____ and danc - ing, The fly - ing hours were filled with

With ne'er a thought ____ to glad - ness, With ne'er a thought of com - ing sad - ness To

dark - en joy - ous youth - ful dreams. With mer - ry sing - ing, with

dark - en joy - ous youth - ful dreams. Sing - ing, with

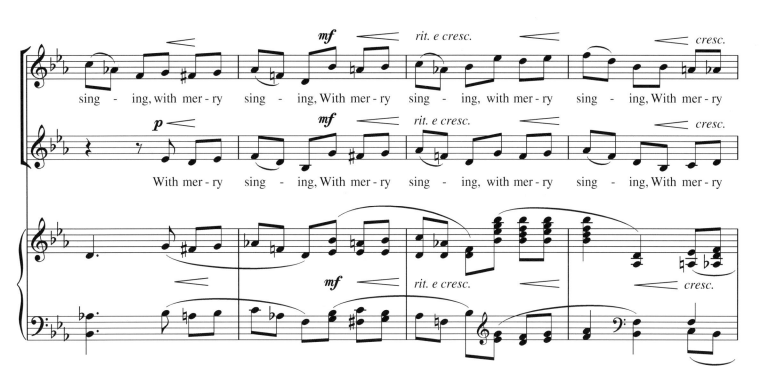

f a tempo / *rit. molto e dim.*

songs _____ and danc - ing, The hours _____ of

songs and danc - ing, The fly - ing hours were filled with

Tempo primo

p

glad - ness. When ___ twi - light weaves her gen - tle spell O - ver

glad - ness. When ___ twi - light weaves her gen - tle spell O - ver

land, o - ver sea, My ___ heart with long - ing turns to

land, o - ver sea, My heart with long - ing turns to

WHO IS SYLVIA?

William Shakespeare

Eric Coates
Arranged by Alec Rowley

mend her? The heav'ns such

mend her? Ho-ly, fair, and wise is she; The heav'ns such

cresc. molto

grace did lend her. That she might ad-mir-ed be,

cresc. molto

grace did lend her. That she might ad-mir-ed be,

rall. *a tempo*

That she might ad-mir - ed be.

rall. *a tempo*

That she might ad-mir - ed be.